MORPHO DIDIUS
Palindromic Poetry

MORPHO DIDIUS
Palindromic Poetry

Rachel Prizant Kotok

ARMATURE PUBLISHING
Providing A Framework For The Language of the Soul

© Rachel Prizant Kotok, 2024

ISBN: 979-8-9857738-2-8

No part of this book may be reproduced, stored in a retrieval system, or transmitted in any form or by any means—electronic, photocopy, recording—without prior written permission from Armature Publishing.

Armature Publishing
c/o Lisa Ferraro
PO Box 254
Worthington, OH 43085
www.armaturepublishing.com
armaturepublishing@gmail.com

Sketches on pp. 49–55 © Rachel Prizant Kotok, 2024

Cover design by Natalia Zukerman

ACKNOWLEDGMENTS

I'd like to thank the following literary homes for these published palindrome poems:

"Seeking Refuge." *Digital Paper*. Issue 25, Fall 2018.

"Eve's Cider," "Danaë's Escape," and "Judith Carries Holofernes's Head." *Hey, I'm Alive Magazine*. Issue 3, Spring 2020.

"Ode: We Kill Like We Do" and "Climate Tipping Point." *Wend Poetry*. Issue 3, Winter 2021.

"What will become of me?"

"There seemed to be no sort of chance of her ever getting out of the room again."

Alice in Wonderland by Lewis Carroll

ABOUT MORPHO DIDIUS

Immersed in subtropical greens, lush emerald to leafy peridot, I stood before the small Catarata La Encantada. The enchanting waterfall flowed into several terraced pools in the steamy basin.

A flash of blue movement in my peripheral vision jolted me. I pivoted, astonished. Hundreds of Peruvian Morpho didius butterflies whirled and spiraled, filling the air with enormous iridescent wings. Facets of shimmering turquoise hues dipped and gyrated as the rare butterflies ascended skyward. Aloft in communal revelry, they soared above the forest and vanished.

For me, Morpho didius represents the potential for transformation and healing. A chrysalis is a sacred space, rendering a significant metamorphosis. Palindromic poetry is a sacred space; I've healed myself through constraints and liberatory writing.

Morpho didius butterflies live for two or three weeks. Let us revel as they do, maximizing our time to heal, enjoy, and create the ever-becoming person one aspires to be.

ORIGIN STORY

As a child, a madman confined me. He threatened my life, and I thought I would die. In my early adulthood, I dared myself to write my way out of continuous mental entrapment. Paradoxically, extreme constrained writing freed me. When I resolved my first palindrome poem, I escaped. The cage door swung open, and wild words ran amok.

ON PALINDROMIC POETRY

Palindrome poems shred and claw prose—this is survivor language. A terse, ungainly idiom has brown dirt under its fingernails. Excavation required.

Palindrome poems are syntactically impolite. Sometimes they babble anachronistically.

Palindromic form forges phoenix-revival from ashy embers. The apex central letter bears Everest witness to the poem's mirrored world.

Palindromic form catalyzes inversion: to be predator and no longer prey. I stalk my own liberation in the tall grasses of language, harming no one.

To the fictional Alice, inquisitive escape artist, and to all Alices who free and heal themselves by any means: Uncork the glass bottle and drink the strange, mirrored language. Palindromic poetry grows curiouser and curiouser!

TABLE OF CONTENTS

Morpho didius palindrome poems

Part 1: Survivor Language

    Trapped   3
    Danaë's Escape   4
    I Am You, Solidarity   7
    Me Too   9
    Judith Carries Holofernes's Head   11
    The Octogenarians Wore Blue Numbers at Shul   13
    Seeking Refuge   14

Part 2: Curiouser and Curiouser

    Eve's Cider   18
    Climate Tipping Point   20
    Ode: We Kill Like We Do   22
    Midnight Conversations   25
    Atonement   27

Part 3: Let the Wild Healing Rumpus Continue

    Kinship   31
    Ceremony   33
    Woven   35
    Sex Is Hexes   37
    Avid Diva   39
    Kapow!   41
    Cosmic Wonder   43
    Seer Trees   45

Part 4: Postscript

    Creating Palindromic Poetry   48
    Judith Carries Holofernes's Head: Prose   50
    Danaë's Escape: Prose   51
    Eve's Cider: Prose   53
    Climate Tipping Point: Prose   54

Part 1:

Survivor Language

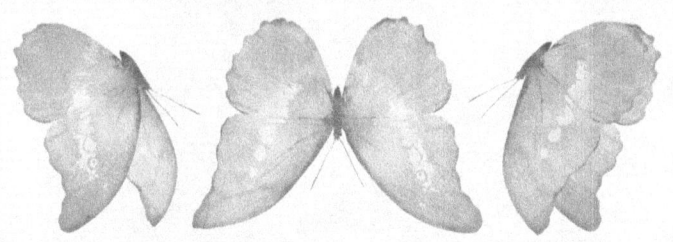

 **TRAPPED**

Devil is sent.
I was a trap.

Y me?

Memory trample.
Hot, ample.

He: "Will I win? In!"
I: "Will I—we—help! Ma!"

To help: martyr-o-me.

Me. My part.
As a witness, I lived.

DANAË'S ESCAPE

Day, Danaë.

Lure, chase:
Nobles' mad maws.

No.

It as secret awe.
Both promised it.

Pure hero, Danaë,
codex ever of rust, iron.

Oh, no.

We spiral
      life buoys
           as you be

    fill a rip
           sew on
                      honor it

Surf ore-vexed ocean,
adore her uptides.

I morph to be water.

Cessation? Swam
damsel bones.

Ah, cerulean!

A dyad.

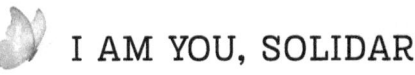 # I AM YOU, SOLIDARITY

Detonate me not.
A slain Eden.
One drags trauma,
i.e., sub alive.

Nod. Rape. **W**e pardon evil. Abuse.

I am U.
Art's garden, one.
Denials? Atone.
Meta-noted.

 ME TOO

war erupts
if none risk
sudden word

sad lotto
or tacit song
all agnostic
at root
told as
drowned dusk

siren on
fist pure
raw

JUDITH CARRIES HOLOFERNES'S HEAD

I
maniac
aloof as time
red now
evil
a maiden-mad flesh
self-damned
I am alive
wonder emits a fool
a Cain
am
I

THE OCTOGENARIANS WORE BLUE NUMBERS AT SHUL

mood

was raw red
nu? devil-rat
ss diva-demon gas
evil eras

we jews
raw time elapses
ire rises pale
emit wars

we jews
are lives
a gnome david's star
lived under warsaw

doom

 **SEEKING REFUGE**

SOS:

nil aid nets.
ill life, no gem.
oh, am I alive?

war trap.
deity meme.

esteem so,
grace.

vast sum,
to helixes,
atoned.

I, hard nut,
sad as tundra.

hide not?
as exile, hot.

must
save
cargos.

meet, see me,
my tied part,
raw.

evil aim,
a home
gone.

fill.
listen.
dial in:

SOS.

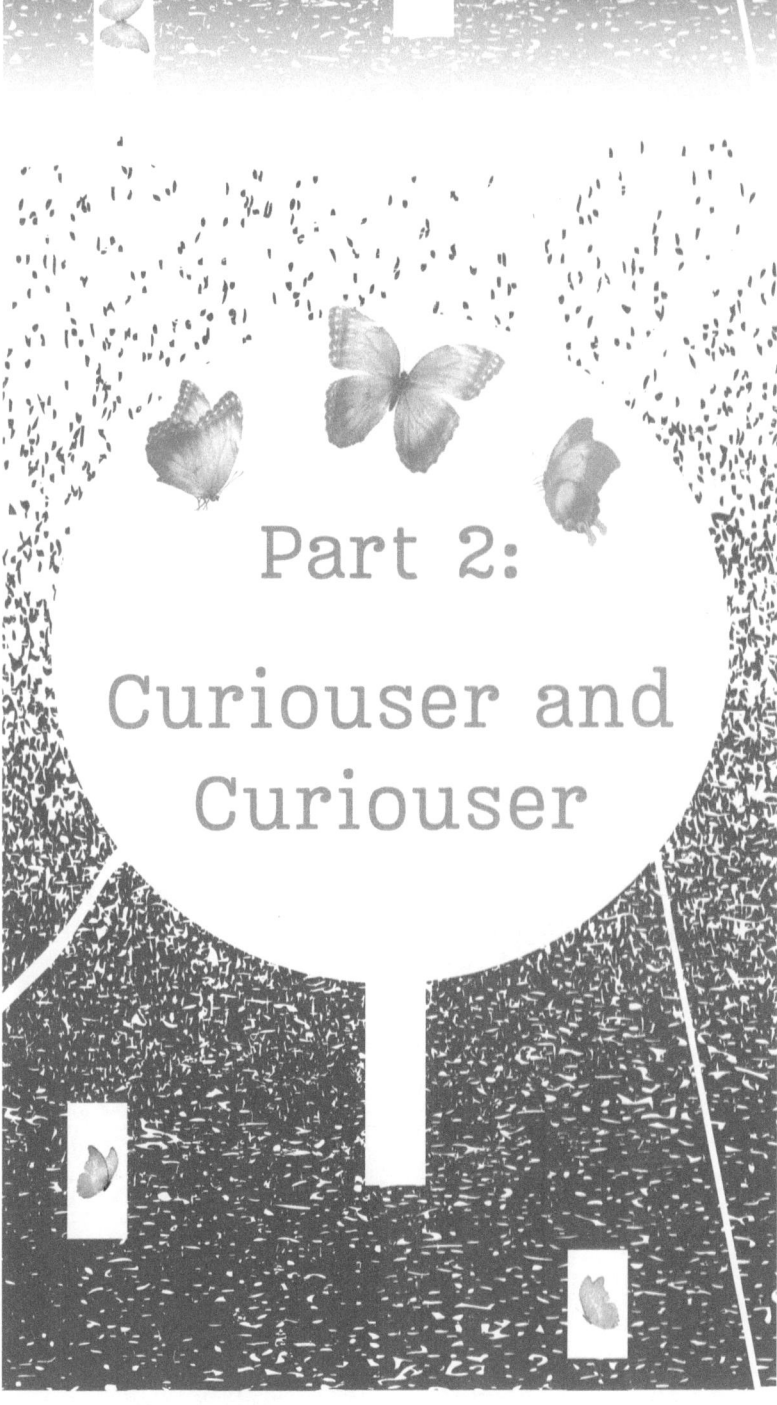

EVE'S CIDER

Yaw alias ERA.
Desire rips as exile.

Hero,
level, rig, demand
nimmed aid.

Sex,
a tie. Vagina.
Maybe damsel
or slag. Nerd.
Omni-trope lame.
Fade.

Garner Eve.

"Egad!"
"No bias!"
"No basis!"

At stasis,
a bonsai bondage.

Ever enraged, a female
port in modern gals.

"Roles made by a man?
I gave it axes."

Diadem mind named Girl;
Eve lore.

Helixes:

aspire
        rise
                dare
        sail
away

CLIMATE TIPPING POINT

Sure-tuned raga now.

Slam in a drowned lore,
wolf mute.

rob
        rain
                models
      drib
drab

Beware.

Virid revel. Bats.

To dire plan, retell.
A seer to speed-devastate sneer.

Got tenets?
Draw notes.

Reviver, set onwards!

Tenet: to green,
set at "saved."

Deep so.

*Trees,
all eternal peridot.*

*Stable Verdi river,
a web.*

*Bard-birds led
omni-arboretum.*

*"Flower,"
olden word.*

*Animals won
a garden uterus.*

ODE: WE KILL LIKE WE DO

MIA:
e.g. Run AWOL. Laws.

Spat sniper:
ifs, nos, buts

Emits tin word:
stole

Soon.
Now.
Anger.

U.S. dire:
grab, loot.

Snug trap.
No code.
We kill like we do.

Con part:
guns = tool

Barge, rid.
Sure.
Gnaw on noose.

Lots drown.
It's time.

Stub sons' fire!

Pins, taps.
Swallow an urge:

Aim.

MIDNIGHT CONVERSATIONS

spill laden words
draught
obsess
older
set one defile mode

Pandora: p**o**p!

a rod, nape, dome
life denotes
red losses
both guards
drowned all lips

ATONEMENT

Mix-a-me.

Garner,
even nod,
rapt.

Pews.
I sat.

Symbol is
Atlas's eyes.

I rise.

Yes, salt
as I lob
my stasis.

Wept.

Pardon,
never enrage.

Maxim.

Part 3:

Let the Wild Healing Rumpus Continue

 **KINSHIP**

wonder casts
a petal idyll

a birth: tri-**m**irth

tribally dilate
past sacred now

 **CEREMONY**

Are we now
to wed?

Forever
of awe,
now two,
new,
a forever
of dew.

O two!
New era.

 **WOVEN**

Muse, rise!
Day o' joy.

Tied yarn,
us, dual.

Wedded. Art
in rows woven.

One vow sworn,
I traded dew.

Laud sunray deity,
O joy!

A desire,
sum.

SEX IS HEXES

Sex, eh?
Meet serial feral fix.
A model lewd yen.
Oh, lever—

P**o**p!

Revel.
Honey dwelled.
O maxi-flare.
Flair: esteem hexes.

AVID DIVA

sex alert
salt

a pure venus
sore

not naive
dare

avid, a
seer

frees a
diva

era deviant on
eros

sun ever
up

at last
relaxes

KAPOW!

hot
lover
spasms
a grow
onsets
a
tacit
ore
erupts

altar of burst love volts!

rub for
at last
pure
erotica
tastes
now
orgasm
saps
revolt
oh

 COSMIC WONDER

Sun, ever a ballet,
ran ultra.

A recipe to plait
selects a vatic,
a tasseled ore, hoary.

Lase cargo, sage **V**ega!
So graces a Lyra.

Oh, erodeless,
a tacit, a vast
celestial pot.

Epic era, art lunar.
Tell a bare Venus.

SEER TREES

       Seer trees. Muse, rise!

       Den.

       I
             am
                        home

                        open
             as
      fire.

       Serif
             sane
                        poem

                        oh
               Maine
      desire.

       Sum.

       Seer trees.

Part 4:

Postscript

CREATING PALINDROMIC POETRY

In my childhood and adolescence, I kept secrets. Deep, monstrous secrets that I couldn't share with others, even with people I adored. To move forward, I smashed a universe-sized horror into an infinitesimal, spiky seedpod. That seedpod burrowed in the remote depths of my psyche until I was ready to seek support as a young adult.

Therapeutic adventures commenced.

My therapist asked me to share my story. I balked; I wasn't keen on prying open the universe-sized horror. Those sweetgum pods impaled fingers.

"Write first, share later," my therapist said.

When I sat down to write, I had no words. Prose vanished, and my childhood confinement surfaced with dread. Emotion and sensory details pervaded, especially imagery of constrained spaces. I was drawn to narratives of other women fighting for their liberation such as Judith, Danaë, and Eve. Sometimes I embodied them, and other times I envisioned their stories.

I seethed, as I imagined they did.

My anger erupted into a searing rage directed toward a man I would never meet again.

In museums, I'd seen various paintings representing the ancient sanguineous story of Judith and Holofernes. To save her people from a disastrous war, Judith seduced General Holofernes, and then cut off his head. Gruesome? Yes.

Did I fantasize about killing the man who entrapped me? Yes.

But as a pacifist, instead, I immersed myself in Judith's story—without prose. I wrote down singular words, naming them and simultaneously writing each in mirrored form.

Evil = live. Saw = was. Wonder = red now.

Small, mirrored words became phrases. Phrases created longer segments, and I stitched them together. The most challenging endeavor was placing affixes, suffixes, and articles to build cohesive phrases and segments. After half a dozen hours, a palindromic poem emerged to reflect a mirrored form of writing with mostly semantic and syntactic integrity.

Creating and resolving my first palindromic poem ultimately burst the seedpod; relief arrived when I wrote my way out of these parameters. A newfound freedom in shredding conventional syntax elated me. After sharing this poem with my therapist, I was open to begin the hard work ahead.

The nine-year-old girl with a palindromic family name no longer keeps secrets. I've liberated myself from concealment; another person's crime is not my shame. My childhood experience is one tiny shard in our collective, devastating societal culture of violence and violation. The tacit norms of maintaining jagged silence undermine empowerment.

I'll share one of my favorite palindromic words: Reviver.

JUDITH CARRIES HOLOFERNES'S HEAD: PROSE

General Holofernes envisions imminent conquest inside his candlelit tent.

Judith enters, removes her heavy cloak, and pours red wine. With mesmeric movement, her sashay shifts air currents.

The General toasts to her beauty. Judith moves closer, noticing the tiny needles rising on his skin. She peers into his eyes, then skims her slender fingers on the back of his thick neck.

The tall, muscular man boasts endlessly about the King of Assyria and their mighty forces. While sharing plans for a siege, he drains several glasses of wine.

You will be victorious, General, she purrs. With downcast eyes, Judith moistens her lips.

Her coy grin makes him smile. She leans next to him, stroking his cheek. The General empties another glass of wine. Slurred words are jumbled, and bloodshot eyes begin to close.

The General falls asleep. Judith puckers her eyebrows; her eyes harden with fury. She raises the sword she has concealed and strikes him. Her fingers close his eyelids before she places the severed head in her basket.

I murdered a man, she murmurs. *Victory is ours.*

Trembling, Judith exits and sees her breath visible against the obsidian sky, abandoning the gore and spatter for someone else to discover.

DANAË'S ESCAPE: PROSE

How could my father lock me up forever?

Frozen, I stood like a marble statue. My new prison was a subterranean bronze chamber. Fear of infinite confinement terrified me, and my entire body began to shudder. A riotous heartbeat pounded inside my chest, and I could barely breathe.

My mother taught me to take long, slow breaths. Eventually, I regulated my breathing. I paced the room, clenching my hands and wondering if I would ever see her again.

I lost my family. I lost the feel of warm sun on my skin. I lost ocean breezes tinged with the scent of wildflowers. I lost my life, but I was still alive. Alone.

Blazing sconces illuminated the space. I touched the bronze walls. Would someone come to replenish the oil or simply abandon me to the deepest darkness?

The almighty King Acrisius had only one child—me. My father left me to die because he believed in an absurd prophecy: Danaë's son will kill his grandfather, the King.

What son? I was a young woman isolated in captivity. No escape.

The injustice enraged me. I curled up in a fetal position on the floor and howled.

***

An impossible glow appeared from the ceiling. Mortar turned liquid, and golden rays seeped out in a slow stream.

I turned my back to the spectral golden rope moving steadily toward me. It seized my ankles and entwined itself around my calves like a vine. The serpentine mass crept up my thighs, pried my legs apart, and pricked my skin with

a thousand shards. The snarl of thunder paralyzed me.
Zeus.

＊＊＊

When I came to consciousness, I surveyed my bruised body. With eyes closed, I envisioned molten gold flowing in and pumping out of a pulsating heart. A golden fetus flashed across my mind's sky like a streaking comet.

After many moons, my belly grew. Every night, I dreamed of a child with miniature fingers and toes, silken earlobes, and flushed cheeks. I sang to the one inside me as I twirled and danced throughout the chamber. All day, I read poetry and told ancient stories to this precious being. I was no longer alone.

My imagination bloomed. I invented my own stories. As a ritual, every morning I conjured the aroma of sage after a rainstorm and the scent of a newborn baby. My child would speak my language, a language of clouds, salt, sea, and sun.

＊＊＊

When our eyes met for the first time, I glimpsed ribbons of our shared future: we will escape from the chamber. The sea gods will carry us, and the sky gods will bless our journey. Cyan and cerulean, our liberation. We are a dyad: Danaë and Perseus. We, like twinned hope and survival, are alive.

EVE'S CIDER: PROSE

Crane, our women's self-defense teacher, says to imagine it's a plane of energy. Her slither of words arouse irrational thinking. In front of me, the one-inch-thick pine board is real. I tell myself that I have grit and purpose.

Two women grip both sides of the board. Behind each, another pair, arms braced to absorb impact. I pretend this square piece of wood is a figment or mirage.

She calls my name. It's my turn; sparks of terror ignites my body. My heart clangs and rattles in my ribcage. Twenty-seven hand bones might survive unshattered.

With laser focus, my right hand transforms into an ax. I lift my arm and inhale a sky of oxygen. The hair-raising crack of splintering wood fibers startles every nerve ending. Shocked and buzzing for a few moments, I float in a liminal space. Until swoosh—an adrenaline rush snaps me to reality—and my feet are grounded. The scent of pine suffuses the space, and wild pandemonium exhilarates me.

Hand in ice bucket now! Crane shouts. Sweaty women roar and shout as they slap high-fives with my left hand. After icing, brazen women surround me with tight hugs. A culminating rite of passage comes to fruition with twenty-seven hand bones intact.

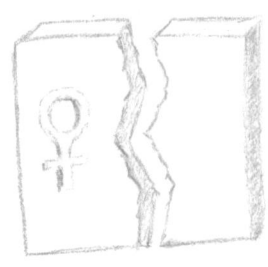

CLIMATE TIPPING POINT: PROSE

An ovoid piercing: tak tak, tak tak. Her raw hunger punctures, shattering the cracked womb. Several days later, light seeps into the blindness. Safe in the nest, illumination stuns with multiple colors.

She moves amidst the shell shards. Ancient, ancestral calcified birth ruins remember. With a feathered thirst, her soft head rises toward the indigo. The first warble sears the newborn throat, a keening trill of emergence.

From the nest, she sees a vast river, wide as light slides into dawn. Her wings tremble and hop with a tentative flutter. A warm breeze rouses desire: she has a yen to taste honeysuckle air midflight. She feels her thudding heartbeat—the joy and ache of being alive.

Once fully fledged, she spreads her wings, surrenders to Icarus lust, and gleans secrets from the wind.

EYE SEES EYE

Thank you, wonderful folks.
I'm deeply grateful for who you are.

Liz Baxmeyer
Neal Colton
Daniel Dyer
María Fellows
Lisa Ferraro
Charles Hacker
Ben Harth
David Kotok
Mitch Kotok
Nivine Kotok
Aisha Kotok
Alison Newell
Sarah Newstok
Scott Newstok
Ruth Newstok
Axel Newstok
Pearl Newstok
Sharon Prizant
Heidi Oline Pruett
Christine Schlessinger
Maggie Sokolik
Regan Stanger
Natalia Zukerman

Dedicated to readers, poets, friends, beloveds, healers, collaborators, artists, and lovers of language.

In memoriam of my first healer, Marcie Mitler.

BIO

Addicted to constrained writing, Rachel writes letter-sequenced palindromic poetry, microfiction, flash, and fiction. She was a finalist for *Southwest Review's* Morton Marr Poetry Prize and the Tucson Festival of Books Literary Award for Poetry. Her work has appeared in *Tiferet Journal, Star 82 Review, Hey I'm Alive Magazine, The Centifictionist, Wend Poetry, Digital Paper* and elsewhere.

www.ingramcontent.com/pod-product-compliance
Lightning Source LLC
Chambersburg PA
CBHW020337010526
44119CB00001B/15